WONDERS!
Our World in Fact and Fiction

FARMS

Sylvia Madrigal

illustrated with photographs

HAMPTON-BROWN BOOKS
Creative Materials for Active Learning

Take a seed.

No, thousands of seeds.

Copyright © 1992 Hampton-Brown Books
All rights reserved. No part of this book may be reproduced or transmitted in any form or by any means, electronic or mechanical, including photocopying, recording or by an information storage and retrieval system, without permission in writing from the Publisher.

Hampton-Brown Books
P.O. Box 223220
Carmel, California 93922

Printed in the United States of America
ISBN 1-56334-069-0

Illustrations: Sharron O'Neil
Photographs: Animals Animals/Earth Scenes: front cover, pp. 1, 2a, 8c, 10, 11, 14a, 14b, 14c, 14d, 16–17, 19b, 21, 23b, 23c; Photo Researchers: pp. 5c, 8a, 8b, 12–13, 14e, 22b, 23a, back cover; Image Bank: 2b, 5a, 9, 16a, 20c; Craig Lovell: 4a; W. D. Murphy/Superstock: p. 3; K. Kummels/Superstock: pp. 6-7; Roger Allyn Lee/Superstock: p. 4b; Grant Heilman/Grant Heilman Photography: pp. 5b, 6b, 20a, 20b, 20e; John Conwell/Grant Heilman Photography: p. 19a; Thomas Hovlandl/Grant Heilman Photography: p. 20d; CA Artichoke Advisory Board: p. 22a; Dan de Wilde: p. 24

Plant them all in the ground,

in row after row.

Add a few special machines and some very important workers.

vacuum seeder

cultivator

harvester

windrower

Be sure there is enough water and sun. And there you have it. Do you know what you've made?

A **vegetable farm!**

Farming is the most important activity in the world. People can't live without food, and almost all the food we eat is grown on farms.

Vegetable farms grow beans and other vegetables: tomatoes, broccoli, carrots, lettuce, and many, many more.

In addition to vegetable farms, there are many other types of farms that produce food. Let's visit some.

DAIRY FARM

Holstein

Cows, cows, and more cows! Do you know where the milk you drink comes from? It comes from milk cows like these.

Guernsey

Jersey

Cows have to eat in order to produce milk. When the pastures are green, cows eat grass. During the fall and winter, they eat **hay**, which is dry grass, or **silage**, a feed made of ground-up corn stalks.

THAT'S A FACT!

A milk cow weighs about 700 kilograms. And she eats some 30 kilograms of feed a day, more than the weight of a six-year-old!

THAT'S A FACT!

Did you know that in one day a cow can give 50 glasses of milk?

1 cow   1 day

And cows like soft music! Some farmers play music in the milking parlor so that the cows will give more milk.

This is a **milking parlor**. Cows have to be milked twice a day. Cows used to be milked by hand, but nowadays there are milking machines.

Even using machines, it takes three hours to milk the 86 cows on this dairy farm.

From Cow to You

1. Raw milk travels through pipes to a storage tank where it is chilled.

2. A truck with a refrigerated tank carries the milk to the dairy.

3. The dairy makes **dairy products**, like butter, cottage cheese, yogurt, and cheese.

4. Another truck carries the products to the market.

Do you like to eat bread and cheese? Well, let's visit a farm where they grow the wheat used to make bread.

WHEAT FARM

This is a field of ripe wheat. It is enormous. Wherever you look, you see golden stalks of wheat.

Some people think wheat is the most important food in the world.

Think of the many things made from wheat: bread, flour tortillas, cereals, spaghetti, and noodles. You probably eat something made from wheat every day.

Grains

Wheat is a grain. These are some of the more important grains.

Wheat

Rice

Oats

Corn

Combines like this one are used to harvest large fields of wheat.

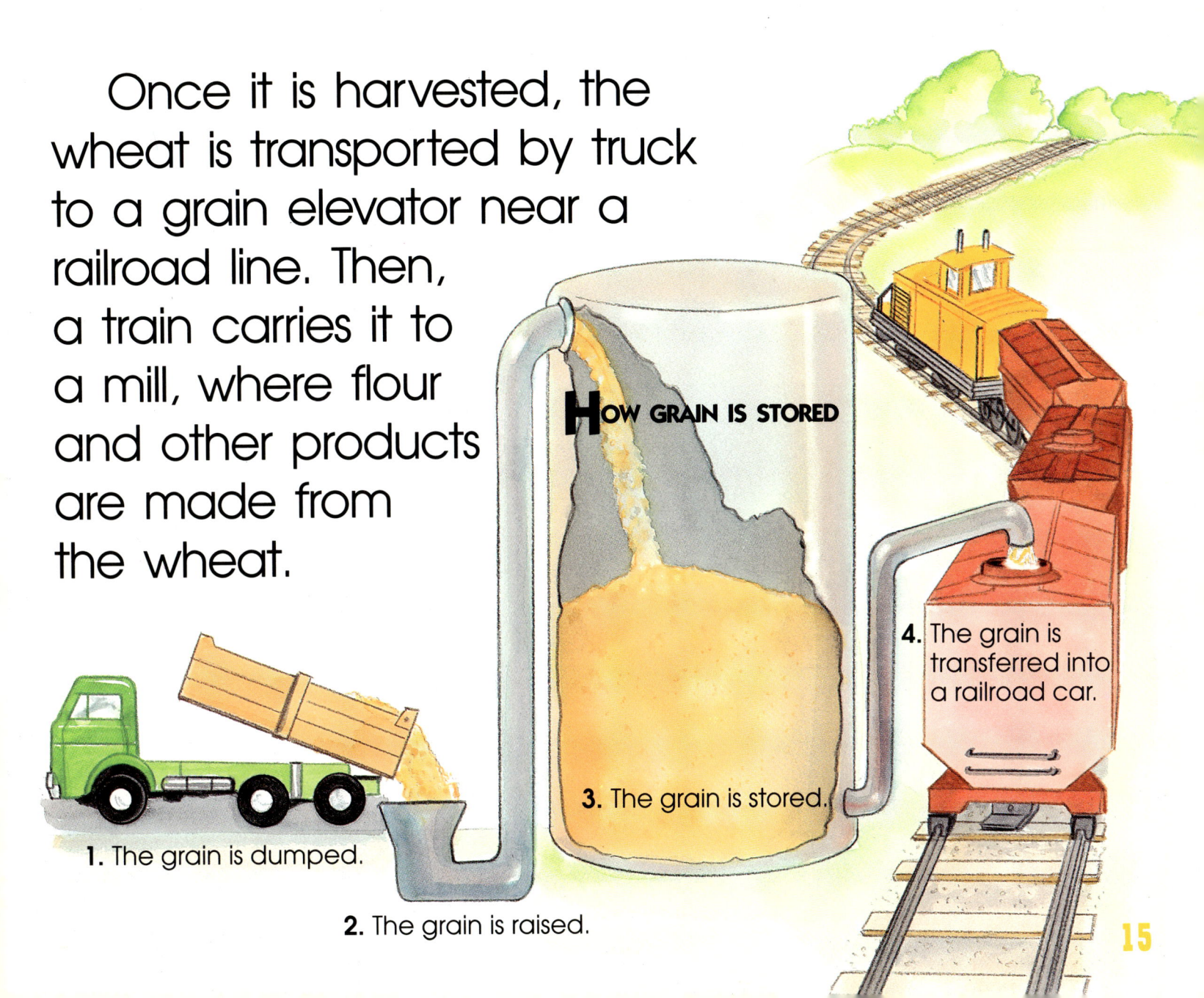

Once it is harvested, the wheat is transported by truck to a grain elevator near a railroad line. Then, a train carries it to a mill, where flour and other products are made from the wheat.

How grain is stored

1. The grain is dumped.
2. The grain is raised.
3. The grain is stored.
4. The grain is transferred into a railroad car.

As you have seen, machines are very important on a wheat farm. On other farms, machines are not as important. Let's visit one of them.

ORANGE FARM

Not much machinery is needed on this orange farm because oranges are harvested by hand. Also, it isn't necessary to prepare the soil and plant every year.

During the harvest, teams of workers pluck the oranges from the trees. They use ladders to reach the ones that are high up.

Hands On

There are two main types of oranges: juice oranges and eating oranges.

Get together with a classmate and observe the two types. Which is larger? What differences do you notice?

Now, peel them. What *other* differences do you notice *between them*? Make a list.

Oranges are grown in regions that have a warm climate. These are the states in the United States that produce the most oranges.

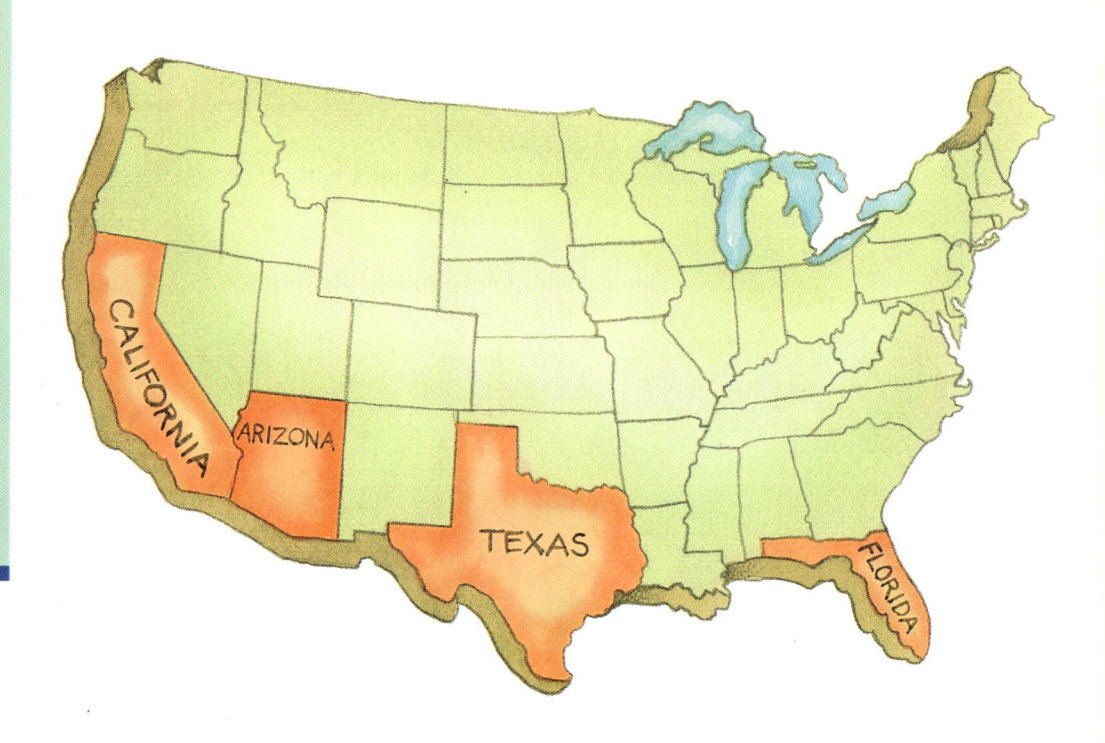

In the warm climates where oranges are grown, there are many insects that can harm orange trees. Farmers spray **insecticides** on their trees to kill insects such as aphids.

Citrus Fruits

An orange is a **citrus fruit**. These are some others.

Lime

Lemon

Tangerine

Grapefruit

After they have been picked, eating oranges are taken to a shed where they are sorted according to size.

Hands On

Though similar on the inside, citrus fruits differ in color, taste, and size. Taste several types and make a chart like this one to compare them.

CITRUS FRUITS	color	taste	size
orange			
grapefruit			
lime			
lemon			
tangerine			

Then the boxes of oranges are loaded in trucks and shipped to markets throughout the country.

All Around the World

All around the world, farming is an important activity. Different plants are raised in different climates.

The cool climate of the central coast of California is suited to growing artichokes.

This banana plantation is in Brazil. Banana trees need a warm climate.

The hot climate of Syria is good for growing peanuts.

In the Philippines, water buffaloes are still used to prepare the rice paddies. The paddies are flooded while the rice plants are small.

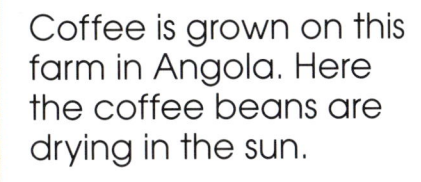

Coffee is grown on this farm in Angola. Here the coffee beans are drying in the sun.

Farms around the world provide us with many things: vegetables, milk, grain, fruit.

No matter what they produce, farms send their products to market, and from the market, to you!